THE BLACK COMPUTER

Survival

GUIDE

BY ENO ESSIEN

Blackk Inkk Research Group

Drawings: Heiji Morishita

Blackk Inkk Research Group
P.O. Box 1682
Emigrant, MT 59027
406-333-4523
510-839-7406

Printed in the United States of America
First Printing April 1992
Second Printing October 1992
10 9 8 7 6 5 4 3 2 1

To "Chief" and "Doc" – my parents –
for all your struggles and all your dreams.

CONTENTS

PREFACE

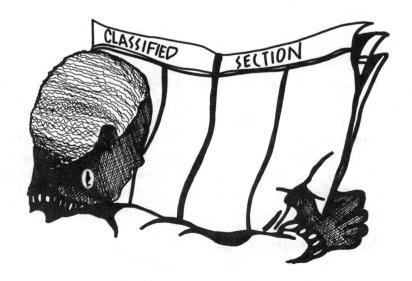

MY STORY

I would be lying if I told you I always liked computers. My first experience with them was typically naive. I felt they were hard to learn and extremely boring. Yet I kept hearing, "Computers are the future, kid" and that if I expected to make it in my generation, I would have to learn them. I went to a High School that had a special computer program, but even after graduation I still did not feel I had obtained any computer skills. The teachers talked over my head, and I just prayed I would pass. As a result, in my early college years I avoided all computer courses and concentrated on parties, football games, and women! Then, at the end of my second year, I ran into a financial disaster. I was evicted from my apartment, my sport car's head gasket blew, and all my creditors were breathing down my neck. I had "expensive taste," and now it was time to face the music.

I knew I had to start making money, and my little odd jobs would not help my situation. I recall going to the job board, hoping to find a good-paying job with only filing and phone answering experience. I quickly learned that many good-paying jobs required computer skills. I was frustrated, but had to pay the rent, and I wanted to satisfy my "expensive taste". So that summer I settled down and learned the "BIG 3" computer applications: Databases (dBASE), Spreadsheets (Lotus 1-2-3), and Wordprocessors (WordPerfect.). I obtained access to a computer, bought simple how-to books on popular computer programs, and found a support group. I returned to school for the fall semester, and instead of crossing my fingers for a good-paying job, I expected it! I was set - jobs came in bunches, bills were paid, and I still have "expensive taste"! After realizing that "the future" is now and computer skills mean money, it took me just a few months to gain computer skills!

SO, WHO SHOULD READ THIS BOOK?

Anyone who feels left out of the computer boom or who simply wants to increase his or her money-making opportunities. Chances are that you are informed about the current computer impact and wonder how to adapt to it. The language in this book is pretty straightforward, and you should not have to run to ComputerLand to find out what something means. The book also has a simple glossary, which you should use to clarify new terms.

The book is geared toward giving you a great snapshot of the personal computer arena for employment while also giving you specific advice and tips on how to quickly and confidently become computer proficient. The IBM PC and PC - compatible computers (I will refer to as simply "PC") are the main focus of the book because they are the most visible in business and dominate the personal computer market.

WHY A BLACK COMPUTER BOOK?

African-Americans are not visibly taking part in America's computer revolution. I think the reason is a lack of a "computer atmosphere" in our communities, rather than lack of intelligence or lack of money. Yes, we see good entry level positions requiring computer skills, but it is difficult to pursue something that is not well received or actively discussed by our own people. This book attempts to bridge the gap between computers and us. There are some African-Americans who are doing quite well in the computer boom, but it becomes much more significant when more of us are getting paid! Unlike current promotional campaigns targeting the African-American community to buy cigarettes and alcohol, there has been no major marketing campaign to sell or promote computers to African-Americans. This is extremely odd when it is a known fact that we are the biggest consumers of electronic items. It is my hope that this book will alert the computer industry to our needs and presence as we prepare to benefit from this booming computer era.

CHAPTER 1

THE BIG 3

Many people are interested in acquiring computer skills, but they do not know where to start. I often hear, "Eno, what do I have to know to make money?" My best answer is "The **BIG 3.**" Most businesses do Wordprocessing, Database and Spreadsheet Management. None of the three is difficult to learn. You probably already know the basics.

WORDPROCESSING

Businesses are like us — we all have to communicate. It should not be a surprise that Wordprocessing is the most popular PC task. The great thing about wordprocessing is that everything you write can be easily changed. So you can type a letter to your mother saying, "I need money, Momma." Then you might realize that you should be more respectful and with a few keystrokes change it to, "Please, Momma, send money," whereas with a typewriter you'd need correction tape, realignment, and a dozen keystrokes to do the job. Also, the **search** and **replace** commands make wordprocessing much more valuable than a typewriter. Let's say you are typing a paper on African-American history. In the paper you type, "Dr. Martin Luther King, Jr." 45 times. Instead, with a Wordprocessing program you can make an acronym like "MLK" and type "MLK" throughout the paper. Then when you finish, you can direct the computer to change (**search and replace**) "MLK" with "Dr. Martin Luther King, Jr."

Wordprocessing skills, coupled with good typing skills, are a valuable combination. Many jobs require just this combination. Go into almost any business, and you are likely to see someone with fast hands and solid wordprocessing skills. Even if you do not know how to type, Wordprocessing is still a good skill to learn. There will be times when you must correspond with people, and a typewriter will be unavailable. Wordprocessing is fairly straight forward and should not be a difficult skill to master.

PC Wordprocessing programs are powerful, and good users know how to get the most out of them. Learning how to produce different types of business documents (letters, memos, charts, mail merge documents, etc.) is a good place to start building wordprocessing skills. Remember, fast typing is not the only qualification for many wordprocessing positions. Just the ability to produce these standard documents (letters, memos, announcements) with a top wordprocessor is often legitimate. But, if by thumbing through your city's want-ads you see typing speed as a major factor, you can take advantage of the educational side of computers. Typing Tutor (Simon & Schuster) and Typing Instructor Encore (Individual Software, Inc.) are software programs known for helping to build speed and accuracy in typing. And you want to know something else? Both programs are fun!

So which wordprocessing software should you learn? In terms of money-making, you should learn the most popular ones. In the business world those are WordPerfect or Microsoft Word. Both are full-featured programs that are standard in all types of businesses. Also, businesses that use other wordprocessor programs may still employ you because you know the best product out there.

There are numerous workshops and user groups to help you learn these packages. Look into it and join one. Also, see about obtaining a copy for yourself. These popular programs list for $400-$500, but it is common for PC users to swipe a copy for half that price.

DATABASES

If you do not know what a database is, I bet some database knows you. We are all in someone's database. If you are college student, you are in your school's database. If you have a credit card, you are in your creditor's database. If you have insurance, you are in your insurer's database. What do they know about you? Everything they need to contact, track, and bill you. Many businesses have databases that are like your phonebook: Name, Address, City, Phone number etc. But business' databases may be more complex: Social Security number, Driver's License number, date of birth, and other identifiable information may also exist in their databases.

Many positions exist for those who can build, maintain, and understand Databases. Sound Hard? O.K. Grab your phonebook. First, you must build a database by defining the **fields**. In a phonebook: Name, Address, City, Phone number are all fields.

Name	Elijah	Name	LaShawn
Address	287 Oak	Address	554 Creek
City	New York	City	New York
Phone #	376-9833	Phone #	666-5433

Once you have entered data into all the fields, you'll have a **record**. To most institutions or businesses we individually are just a record of information. By pulling up our record they can contact us or send us information.

One appreciated feature of a Database is its organizational capabilities. Most of us have our phonebooks in alphabetical order. By thumbing through we can search for names like "Elijah" and "LaShawn." Businesses have larger databases and, therefore, may need to have their Database in alphabetical order, Zip Code order, or City order so they can quickly find a **record** with limited information. For instance, when your account number is missing on a check that you sent to pay the phone bill, the phone company may use another sorted field, for example, your Last Name, to pull up your record in alpha-order to credit your account.

Another common use for business Databases is selecting records with specific criteria. For example, a large corporation may want to send a letter to New York residents announcing its new office in New York. They can use their Database to pull up all their customers in the Big Apple and produce a mailing list.

The most popular Database software programs are **dBASE**, **Paradox**, and **Fox Base**. dBASE is probably the best one to learn first, mainly because it has been the industry's leader for the longest. But the competitors are also good, and if you learn one, you can easily learn them all!

SPREADSHEETS

Spreadsheets are most popular in financial areas (banks, accountants, etc.). Spreadsheets can be used by anyone who uses numbers or has a budget. Let's take a simple scenario.

You have $500, and your expenses are:

Air Jordans	$120
Pay-Back Mom	$150
Car Insurance	$ 75
Movie Tickets	$ 10
Gas	$ 10
Sister's Gift	$ 30
Total Expense	**$395**

And you want to put the remaining portion in the Bank

$500	**My money**
-$395	**My expense**

Savings Account $105

Now, suppose there is a sale on Air Jordans, and the price is now $90 a pair. You can then recalculate.

Total Expense is now only $365.

How much goes into savings now? $135.

One of the joys of Spreadsheet Management is that you may do all the recalculation with one keystroke! How? Let's transfer your budget to a Spreadsheet.

	A	B	C	D
1	Air Jordans	$120	My Money	$500
2	Pay-Back Mom	$150	Savings	$105
3	Car Insurance	$ 75		
4	Movie Tickets	$ 10		
5	Gas	$ 10		
6	Sister's Gift	$ 30		
7	**Total Expense**	**$395**		

The above display is called a Worksheet. This is the area of a Spreadsheet where your data is displayed. As you can see, a Spreadsheet is organized by **columns** (indicated by letters A to D) and **rows** (indicated by numbers 1 to 7). We have entered amounts and text in the **cells.** A specified row and column show a cell. For instance, cell "A7" contains "Total Expense" and cell B2 contains "$150." How was Total Expense (cell B7) calculated? By using formulas. A formula adding cells B1, B2, B3, B4, B5,B6 will compute the Total Expense. Spreadsheet formulas vary: in Lotus 1-2-3 a user would enter "@SUM(B1..B6)." A formula can also compute "Savings". In our example, "My money" (D1) minus "Total Expense" (B7) equals "Savings" (D2). A formula in Lotus 1-2-3 would place "+D1-B7" in the D2 column to compute "For Savings."

Using a Spreadsheet, let's see what happens when Air Jordans go on sale:

	A	B	C	D
1	Air Jordans	$ 90	My Money	$500
2	Pay-Back Mom	$150	Savings	$135
3	Car Insurance	$ 75		

4	Movie Tickets	$ 10		
5	Gas	$ 10		
6	Sister's Gift	$ 30		
7	**Total Expense**	**$365**		

When the price of Air Jordans changes, "Total Expense" and "Savings" also change. In a Spreadsheet, both formulas can be calculated at once. In businesses this multiple calculation feature is critical. In a large company, a single change in a value may effect everything from the company's annual income to the month's payroll.

This is how a Spreadsheet works, and if you have a budget you immediately may become a proficient user. I actually thought that Spreadsheets were the easiest Big 3 application to learn because they often deal with money. And I had so much money trouble that it made sense in a hurry! Those who know Accounting or Bookkeeping have an extra advantage because businesses hire people to manage Accounts Payable and Accounts Receivable by computer Spreadsheet. Just as it is good to have solid typing skills in wordprocessing, it is also good to know Bookkeeping or Accounting. Those who do not know accounting can either take an accounting course or purchase an educational accounting program. I did not know Accounting or Bookkeeping when I first learned Spreadsheet Management, but I still found jobs. Data entry jobs exist for those who know how to operate a Spreadsheet. So, whatever your background is, I recommend that you learn Spreadsheet Management. The Spreadsheet programs which are most visible in Business are **Lotus 1-2-3** and **Microsoft Excel**.

INTEGRATED PACKAGES

The prices of these popular software packages range from $250-$500 each. For some of us this may be a little too steep. Though many jobs may request these specific applications, it still may be in your best interest to try to learn the Big 3 basics in cheaper packages. Lotus 1-2-3 is not the only Spreadsheet, nor is dBASE the only Database you can use to learn Spreadsheets and Database management. A good option is to look into **Integrated Packages**. These are packages that combine the different applications. A couple of popular integrated packages are **Microsoft Works** and **PFS First Choice.** They include a word-processor, database, spreadsheet, and communication program (communications is specifically discussed in the "Your Own Thang" and "Buying Your Own" chapters). They retail for less than $150, and both are very powerful. They will definitely teach you the more important Big 3 basics that are needed to "get paid" at a bargain price.

CHAPTER 2

MO' WAYS TO GET PAID

Wordprocessing, Database Management, and Spreadsheet Management are the most popular PC tasks in businesses. But it is not the only way to get paid. The Big 3 are simple, but very common. Instead you may prefer tasks that are more personal, flexible or even more challenging. Here are a few avenues that you may want to explore.

DESKTOP PUBLISHING

If I were to write this book a year from now, I probably would include Desktop Publishing in the BIG 3 chapter and call it the "Big 4". The popularity of Desktop Publishing is soaring. Desktop Publishing involves integrating or mixing text and graphics together. Before Desktop Publishing, if you wanted to include graphics in a text document it was a hassle. One would use a wordprocessor for text and a graphics program for graphics. Mixing the two together was a disaster. Now, with Desktop Publishing, producing graphic documents is easier. Desktop Publishing created a new phenomenon! It allows you to put a graphic on a page and places text neatly around it.

In addition, Desktop Publishing is popular because of its versatility. It is being used to create everything from technical books to party fliers. Businesses are using it to prepare detailed reports, newsletters, and announcements. It is tremendously popular among graphic artists, resume services, and self-publishers. The most popular Desktop Publishing programs are **Pagemaker** and **Ventura**. These are the ones you will likely see in many businesses and will be requested by employers. Like most popular software programs, Ventura and Pagemaker are not cheap. Desktop Publishing programs like **Publish it!** and **Express Publisher** are two good, fairly inexpensive Desktop publishing programs. They are great for learning Desktop Publishing basics and doing simple tasks.

If you are the artistic or the creative type, Desktop Publishing is definitely something to investigate. If you are not, like me, look into taking a basic class in graphic design or get a simple Desktop Publishing book. Although Desktop Publishing can be fun, it does require some artistic judgement to be effective. Besides giving you a job-hunting skill, Desktop Publishing can help create a business. Business cards, professional resumés, business letterheads, African-American newsletters, and hundreds of other services and products are created with Desktop Publishing.

TECHNICAL SIDE

If you have ever had your car, stereo, or television repaired or serviced, you know somebody who is making good money. The popularity of personal computers has increased the need for computer technicians. It is not extremely hard to become a PC technician either. PC Technicians usually are not required to be Engineers or have college degrees. It is common to see High School kids fixing PCs at local computer dealerships. Why is that? Well, inside the PC is a relatively simple machine. If there is a problem, you can almost immediately isolate it. For instance, all the major components (monitor, disk drive, printer) are connected to cards. If something goes wrong, Technicians can search for the appropriate card, then either replace the cable or card. This is a simple but common example of PC technical issues. It is not always this simple, but if you like working with your hands, this could definitely be your avenue. One Black technician told me he has more trouble putting in car stereos than fixing PCs. Computer outlets are always demanding good PC technicians. Salaries range from $8/hr-$20/hr. Good and experienced technicians command higher salaries. It's not outrageous for these technicians to earn wages in the $40/hr-$80/hr range.

To break into the technical arena, the best thing to do is to take a PC Technician class. Check computer magazines for these courses. Or you may just have the knack to teach yourself.

A lot of technicians just like to "fiddle with things" and easily learned PC repair. So, buy a book to guide you through the basics of PC repairing or upgrading. If there is not a computer bookstore near you, go to Waldenbooks, Crown Books, or B. Dalton and head for the computer section.

PROGRAMMING

Programming is probably the part of computers you have heard the most about. If you have taken a computer course, more than likely it was a programming course. Almost everything is programmed in the computer arena, from the chips inside your PC to your wordprocessor. They all have instructions coded inside that perform specific operations. If you like to create or are fond of figuring out puzzles, you may want to look into programming.

Let's build a scenario. You need a program to compute the tax on an item in your new business. You cannot just type into a computer, "What's my sales tax?" You need to use a programming language to translate it into a language a computer can understand. BASIC is the language most schools teach since it is geared toward beginners. Let's look at a BASIC program that computes sales tax on a $100 sale.

```
NEW
10 SALE = 100
20 SALES.TAX = SALE * .06
30 PRINT "The tax on your item is ";SALE.TAX
RUN
```

The result:

```
The tax on your item is 6
```

Explanation

First, the amount of the sale is defined and assigned to a variable, "SALE = 100." Second, the sales tax is calculated, "SALE * .06." This formula is also assigned to a variable, "SALE.TAX = SALE * .06." Line 30 is the only line that will be displayed to the user. It also includes the computed sales tax (SalesTax).

DATABASE AND C PROGRAMMING

The other programming languages are more challenging and are in other arenas besides the educational sector. Database programming is geared towards businesses. dBASE IV and the other top database programs have programming languages that let you take greater control over Database design. C is the programming language that is used by many PC professional programmers. Everything from games to your typing program is most likely programmed in C.

What should you learn? If you have no or little programming experience, start with BASIC or Pascal, but I might as well tell you that the money is in database programming and C. Businesses often need Customized Databases and will gladly pay $15/hr-$40/hr.

What is a Customized Database? It is a database that has been programmed to automate tasks that a business or an individual does regularly. Businesses want to make computers easier to use for their employees. For instance, a Data Entry Clerk may work on a Customized Database that has only menus and screens that focus on a particular tasks. Instead of a Clerk knowing how to operate dBASE IV, his Customize Database has menus to help guide the Clerk. One sister I know selects "mail" from her database menu every morning to get into her mail entry screen, and types "labels" to print out mailing labels in the evening. Businesses pay big money for those who are good at programming Customize Databases. How do you learn to program Customize Databases? The more powerful Database programs like dBASE and Paradox have special programming languages and an extensive programming manual. So, while you are learning Database basics, it's a good idea to explore programming them also.

C programming is the preferred computer language of most professional programmers. How do you learn C? There are classes on the subject, but many people also pick it up on their own. There are software packages available like Microsoft QuickC. This, combined with one of the hundreds of books available on C, will introduce and guide you through C programming. If you become proficient in C, you can write your own software and sell!

CHAPTER 3

FINDING COMPUTERS

The best place to find, use, and learn about computers cheaply and extensively is at a school. **Universities, Community Colleges,** and **Adult Schools** have computer classes that teach relevant computer skills. If you are a college student, then you can easily add a computer course to your schedule. (See "School Daze!" chapter for more on students.) If not, for a small enrollment fee the Public Community Colleges and Adult Schools have classes that usually include access to a computer lab. What if you have a 9:00 to 5:00 job? Community Colleges and **University Extension** programs have evening and weekend classes that are convenient for day workers. University Extension programs are held at major Universities, and classes are open to the public. **Trade/Technical Schools** are also popular, but the cost of attendance could be thousands of dollars. They have resources similar to University and Community College settings and boast great job placement opportunities. **Private Training Services** give you more individual attention, but most charge high hourly rates. Here, training tends to be in smaller groups or even one-on-one. Also, check **Computer magazines** for listings of Big 3 classes.

Also, if you work for a big company, check your benefit package. Your employer may pay for your outside computer courses. One African-American long-distance phone company employee I know said she found out accidently that computer education was part of her employee benefit package. So on weekends, at her company's expense, she attended an outside computer education center.

Remember, in most of these educational environments it is up to you to get what you pay for. Many instructors will get paid whether you learn or not, so it is important that you press them for knowledge. Too often I hear friends say that the teacher was "too much of an intellectual," and they proceeded to lose interest in the subject entirely. If this is the case, cut through the hype and let the instructor know what you do not understand.

Many teachers are just very excited about their subject, but have difficulty teaching it. My first computer teacher was an elderly man who, on the first day, said, "Computers don't make mistakes, people do." This was the only thing I understood through the entire course. He had a great deal of computer knowledge, but he sure did not pass any of it on to me!

CHAPTER 4

COMPUTER ATMOSPHERE

Even if you attend the best school, get the Big 3, and purchase a fast PC, you may still have difficulty becoming a sound PC user. A good way to boost your computer expertise is to meet people who can better help you understand PCs. I will be the first to tell you that it is hard to learn computers when there is nobody besides instructors to talk to about them. Most strong computer users have some type of arena besides the educational sector they use as a resource to help boost their computer literacy. It may be a group of friends or co-workers on the job whom they use for computer support. You, too, should seek out an atmosphere - beside schools - that will help you become a sound computer user.

USER GROUPS

Computer User Groups are a great arena to seek out help to build your computer expertise. Nobody knows everything about computers, but User Groups serve as an arena in which you can ask many different people various questions. There all sorts of Computer User Group from Basic Beginners to specialized groups for doctors and lawyers. Computer User groups also can help you obtain computers and software. Computer vendors love to target support groups for promotion and big sales. For instance, Software makers like Lotus may come and do demonstrations and pass out free copies of their latest package. Larger user groups, like the San Francisco PC Group or the Boston Computer Society, may regularly have these special events, but even smaller groups can benefit new users. You never know who you will meet, and help you buy a computer or even help you find a job!

Where do you find User Groups? First, check out the computer retail stores. Computer User Groups usually post meeting announcements there. Other places to check are libraries and colleges for postings. And definitely ask around - chances are something will be right for you. If not, start one!

You do not need Congress' approval or a letter from IBM to begin a User Group. Get a group of people with similar interests, arrange meeting times, and "break it down."

ON-LINE SERVICES

If you have a computer, you can use a **modem** to dial up On-line services. What is a modem? It is a device that makes your computer act like a telephone and call up other machines. (More on modems in "Buying Your Own" and "Your Own Thang.." chapters). Many On-line services feature User Groups as part of their services. On-line Services like **Prodigy** have forums where you can ask other users questions. Topics include everything from buying a computer to saving tips and tricks in popular software programs. I liked On-line Services a lot because I could ask dumb questions without anyone ever seeing me. I became comfortable because people would write back, giving me all kinds of ideas and suggestions.

THE BDPA

The Black Data Processing Associates (BDPA) is a group African-American professionals who have formed an attractive arena for computer users and technical people. They provide computer workshops, job listings, networking, and offer support in developing computer literacy. They believe that computer literacy must be addressed by African-American people. The BDPA is showing that computer skills is also a "BLACK THANG," and for many African-Americans it has made the computer revolution easier to deal with. I knew I would join the organization after the first meeting I attended, mainly because I felt very comfortable discussing computers and other social developments concerning African-Americans. It seemed that we were all on the same page, and I met people with similar backgrounds. The BDPA is a nationwide organization; a listing of chapters is provided in Appendix A.

Also, the BDPA circulates chapter and national Newsletters, so you can keep in touch with all the organization's developments. Annual membership is only $75, and only $15 for students. Definitely check them out!

MAGAZINES

The computer boom has generated hundreds of computer magazines. This is also a good place to boost your computer literacy. Many newsstands carry the popular computer magazines for just a few bucks per copy. I must admit for a novice or beginner some may be hard to get into. Many may seem way too advanced. **PC World** is a good one to cuddle up with; it will keep you up to date in plain English. Another good magazine is **PC Novice**. **PC Novice** is geared for the beginner and has loads of information on common questions, like "What computer should you buy?" to "How to copy multiple files?" For more information on magazines, see Appendix B.

CHAPTER 5

ON THE INSIDE

ANATOMY OF PC

This is the part of computers that usually puts us to sleep. Talking about parts of a PC may be exciting to a computer fanatic, but for the average user it is just passing time. However, there are a few parts of the PC that are of interest, and this section will help you better understand the equipment. Also, a good understanding of the anatomy may open several avenues for you to get paid (see "Mo Ways" chapter)

MICROPROCESSOR

This is the brain of a computer, sometimes called the "computer on a chip." Every function, task, or job your computer does runs through the microprocessor. Another name for the microprocessor is the Central Processing Unit (CPU). As you may have guessed, the "brain" is a hot topic in the computer world. Computer developers are always trying to find ways to make it faster or make it do tasks more efficiently - or simply add more "brain power." In 1981, PC discussion revolved around the 8088 chip. In early 1992, the lightning quick 80486 chip is the hot topic. As a buyer, you should know that the PC microprocessor type is a big determinant of price. As a user, the type of microprocessor mainly means speed. The speed of the microprocessor is measured in Megahertz (Mhz). (Megahertz measures the clock rate speed of the CPU). Technically, the faster the microprocessor speed (or the higher megahertz), the faster the PC will operate. Here is a quick table on the development of the PC Microprocessor:

CPU	Year Introduced in PC	Computer	Mhz
8088	1981	PC XT	4.77-12 Mhz
80286	1984	PC AT or "286"	10-16 Mhz
80386	1985	"386"	20-33 Mhz
80386SX	1988	"386SX"	16-33 Mhz
80486	1989	"486"	25-33 Mhz

MEMORY

Computer memory may be the easiest part of computer anatomy to understand. The "brain" needs memory to store information before and after it processes it. In the computer arena Memory is primarily known as RAM or Random Access Memory. RAM is only available when the computer is on, and is mainly used to load programs and temporarily hold information for the microprocessor to process. In the computer world memory is measured in Bytes, Kilobytes, Megabytes... What is this? Well, a byte is any single character like "1". Now look at the chart :

Byte	Kilobytes or K	Megabytes or Mb
Single character like "1"	1000 bytes	1,000,000 bytes
One "1"	1000 "1"	1,000,000 "1"

PC memory is also a big determinant of a PC's price, computer speed, and capabilities. Software packages have become larger. Now more memory is required to run newer programs. The first IBM PC machines had only 256K; now 1 megabyte is becoming the standard.

FLOPPY DRIVES AND DISKETTES

Remember that memory is available for holding information only when the computer is on. Where does the information go when you turn off the computer? This is where storage comes in. The PC contains drives for users to store information.

The first PCs featured only 5.25" disk drives. This means that information could be stored only on 5.25" diskettes.

Now the 3.5" disk drives are available for the PC, and 3.5" diskettes can be used to store information.

Both sizes can be obtained in **high density** and **double density** formats. What is the difference? Basically, the amount of information it can store. (We measure memory the same way we measure storage.)

How much data can a diskette hold?

Disk Size	Double Density	Typed Pages	High Density	Typed Pages
5.25"	360 K	180	1.2 Megabytes	600
3.5"	720 K	360	1.44 Megabytes	722

Though the 5.25" diskette has been a part of the PC world longer, the 3.5" is becoming more preferred. Besides storing more information, it also has a harder exterior. The 5.25" diskette is flexible and can easily be disfigured. Losing information because of damaged diskettes is the worst nightmare for any computer user !

HARD DISKS

PC makers anticipated early that programs will become larger and people will have more data to store. Users could not be limited to storing all their data exclusively on floppy diskettes. Over the years, hundreds or even thousands of diskettes could result! One reason the **Hard Disk** or **Fixed Disk** was created was to deal with this issue. Hard Disks are bigger and heavier than floppy disks. They usually are "fixed" inside a PC and, unlike Floppy disks, are not transportable. Hard Disks come in different storage sizes. Home users may be content with 20, 40, or even 80 megabyte Hard Drives, while large businesses may have 100 Megabytes to 1 Gigabyte (100,000,000 bytes) Hard drives.

Disk Size	Typed Pages
20 Megabytes	10,000
40 Megabytes	20,000
80 Megabytes	40,000
100 Megabytes	50,000
I Gigabyte	500,000

MOTHERBOARD

The motherboard is the circuitry board in the PC that contains all the components that run the computer. The microprocessor, memory chips, floppy disks controller cards, hard disk drive controller cards, and other vital components are all "plugged" or connected to the motherboard. You may think of the motherboard as the foundation of a PC. If you decide to do a major **upgrade,** like changing to a faster microprocessor, the motherboard most likely also will change to support the new microprocessor.

ANATOMY...

Now you know the basic parts. So, when you hear those computer nerds talking about their fast microprocessor or the size of their Hard Disk capacity, you will know it is not such a big deal. But listen in – you might be able to tell them a few things they forgot!

CHAPTER 6

BUYING
YOUR OWN

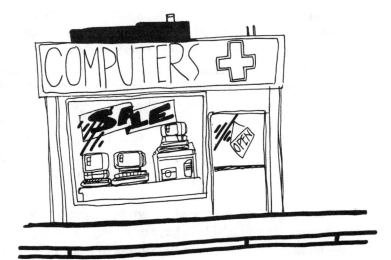

To become PC-literate, I strongly suggest you buy a PC. There is nothing like learning in your own home and on your own time. Yes, it is fine to take computer classes, but your own system is the best investment. "Computers cost too much!" I hear this all the time, and it usually comes from those with $150 shoes, 25 inch televisions, "boomin'" systems, leather trench coats, or the leased sports car! A computer is an investment that can give you more returns than all these things (and let you buy the car instead of leasing it!). Once you gain computer skills, chances are that the computer will pay for itself. My computer is worth about $800, but it has been paying rent and monthly bills for the last few years - and has left money to burn!

I maintain that no matter what your budget is, it is possible for you to obtain a PC. I should also tell you that buying a PC can be as complex as buying a car, or as simple as getting fast food, depending on what you know. Every time a newer model PC comes out, it usually drives down prices of the existing PCs. You can get a basic system for under $500 and still develop computer skills.

Remember the "On The Inside" chapter? If you recall those important parts of a PC, it will greatly assist you in determining which PC is affordable and right for you. However, there are other factors, like peripherals, manufacturers, and price, that will make your decision unique. For instance, if you are a new user, do not spend time gazing at the latest, greatest, fastest microprocessor on the market. Find something that gets the job done. If you just want to learn the Big 3 (Wordprocessing, Database Management, and Spreadsheet Management), the earlier model PCs, such as the PC XT or PC AT, will suit you fine. Also, ask yourself what you plan to be doing in a couple years. If you expect your PC tasks to grow, make sure you buy a PC that is easily upgradable to later models. For example, buy a PC that has a case which can easily support a new motherboard with a faster microprocessor.

THE CLONE IMPACT

Besides being a nickname, there is another reason why I have referred to IBM PC computers as simply "PC." That reason is that IBM is not the only "PC" maker. Yes, IBM introduced the standard version of the PC in 1981. However, IBM did not use or create any new technology in building the PC. This made it possible for other companies also to build PCs. **AT & T, Zenith, Hewlett-Packard** are some big name companies that also build PCs. These computers are called IBM compatibles, clones, or DOS-based computers (they also use the DOS operating system). The clone impact has not only changed the way IBM compatibles are referenced, but they have also driven down prices. Clone computers are often cheaper than IBM PC, but IBM usually has better support services (repair, warranties, etc). Businesses are generally high on IBM because of support. Individuals tend to buy "clones" because they are cheaper. So, as a potential consumer you have options. But in your decision-making, do not buy IBM because it is the "original" or "the real McCoy," and do not overlook clones because they are "imitations" or "copy cats." Generally, they both do the same thing. Explore the options. If you are a student, it may not hurt to buy IBM, because IBM offers great student discounts (See Student chapter for more info). But even as an aware, ordinary shopper, you will come across some top notch clone makers that offer excellent support service.

WHAT TO BUY?

There is not one perfect computer system for everyone. So, before you choose ask yourself some questions. "What kind of work will I do?" "Will I need a lot of memory?" "Do I want to expand in a few years?" These are some of the questions that will make your decision totally unique. Let's look again at the essential parts of a PC.

MICROPROCESSOR

The type of microprocessor you choose will be a big determinant of price. Therefore, you should carefully analyze your needs. If you just need to learn the Big 3 or only want to do basic PC computing, then a **low end** microprocessor (8088 or 80286) would be legitimate. However, if you plan to do more sophisticated tasks like complex scientific calculations or graphics, a **high end** (80386, 80486) microprocessor is more appropriate. Remember, a microprocessor is a big factor in determining a PC's speed. A novice should not be concerned with getting a super quick microprocessor because his or her work will not require one.

MEMORY (RAM)

Someone once told me that you can never have too much memory. Even when dealing with PCs, this is still true. More memory allows you to run larger programs and (along with the microprocessor) also works to speed up your PC's performance. The industry's standard is 640K, but it is rapidly approaching 1 Megabyte or Mb. Try to obtain a system that has at least that much memory. 512K machines are also available and run a sufficient number of programs, but you may encounter problems running some of the newer applications. When searching for a PC, check to see if you can expand the memory. For instance, some systems come with 1 Mb of memory but may be expandable to 2, 4, 8 or even 32 Mb! Additional memory is fairly cheap, so this may help you not to"grow out" of your machine too soon.

FLOPPY DISKS

You are going to have to decide what kind of storage devices you want. Floppy disks are a must, but the size and quantity is up to you. Two **5.25" disk drives** was the standard in the early 1980s. Now people are removing one 5.25" floppy drive and replacing it with a **3.5" floppy drive**. Then there is the issue of density. Remember that high density disk drives read both high density diskettes and double density diskettes. Double density disk drives can only read double density diskettes. If you can buy both 3.5" and 5.25" high density drives, you are in business. If you get double density drives, you may stumble into a few problems if software makers do not provide double density versions. Recall that double density diskettes do not hold as much data, and it generally costs software makers more money to ship more diskettes.

HARD DISKS

"What size?" Is the big question here. In the early 1980s, PC users boasted **10 Mb Hard Drives**, but now they boast about ten times that amount. Which one is right for you? It depends on your needs. But a good size is a **40 Mb Hard Drive**. If you do not have much to store, 20 Mb is legitimate. Because more and more applications are requiring a Hard Disk to run, the Hard Drive, which used to be optional, is becoming an essential part of PC computing.

MONITORS

In deciding what monitor to buy, you will again have to analyze your needs. Color monitors are everyone's favorite, but they are also the most expensive. A good affordable monitor is a **color VGA** (Video Graphics Adapter). This is especially nice for those who are high on graphics or games. If you are strictly business (the Big 3), a monochrome, or "one color," will be just fine. **Monochrome monitors** do not display graphics and are really a fine consumer's option. The price of a standard size (14") monochrome monitor can run as low as $80, while a color VGA starts at around $350. But wait! There is a middle ground - the **monochrome VGA**! The display, while in one color, does display graphics. It is cheaper than a color VGA, but more expensive than a monochrome. This is an avenue that many, including me, have chosen!

THE COMPLETE PC, HOW MUCH $?

Most PC users do not buy their PC piece-by-piece, but buy a complete machine. Disk drives, Hard Drives, Monitors, Memory, and other PC parts will already be configured for the users. However, you should use your main components preferences to guide you in making your decision. Definitely ask yourself what is affordable, because "wants" and "finances" do not always match. For my first few years of PC computing I pounded on a basic PC XT (8088) clone with a monochrome monitor with two floppy drives, and later I added a Hard Drive. I learned the Big 3, DOS, and even a few technical things about my PC. The whole system was worth about $550 tops. My computer nerd friends would laugh when they saw my machine, but I didn't care as long as it was getting me to the bank!

Besides the computer maker, the features (drives, how much memory, type of monitor) surrounding the microprocessor make computer prices vary. An **AT** or **286** PC may range from $500-$1700. A 386 computer will fall into the $1000 - $4000 range. There is also a **386SX,** which is a stripped down version of the 386. The 386SX is very popular option because it provides some 386 features at prices competitive to the 286. The 386SX prices generally range from $850 -$2000.

If money is still a question, check into financing a computer. Again, a computer is a solid investment that will return more than just money! Companies like **Dell Computers** offer financing options for buyers to help obtain their top-notch systems.

WHERE TO BUY?

There are five primary channels to buy computers:

1) Authorized Dealer
2) Manufacturer Direct
3) Value Added Resellers
4) Mass Consumer Stores
5) Mail Order

Just as there are car dealers, there are also computer dealers. **Authorized Dealers**, like ComputerLand, are the people who have a direct relationship with the manufacturer. Authorized dealerships also sell most of the computers on the market. **Manufacturer Direct** is buying directly from the producer (in other words, cutting out the middle man). This is also popular, but unless you live near the manufacturer you would have to purchase the system by mail. But, this source offers a warranty, and people are finding savings with this method. **Value Added Resellers (VARs)** are companies that buy from the manufacturer, enhance the machine in some way (i.e., add a color monitor), and then sell it again. **Mass Consumer** stores like Sears make arrangements with computer manufacturers to sell their systems. **Mail Order** companies usually offer the lowest prices because they generally have lower operating costs than the other four and survive on small profits.

On the whole, there is nothing wrong with buying through any of these channels, but all buyers are not the same. For instance, if you know exactly what you want and can manage without having the manufacturer around the corner, buy Mail Order or Manufacturer Direct, and save. On the other hand, if you feel that you want visible and steady support, contact your nearest Authorized Dealer and they will take care of you.

PERIPHERALS

Printers

If you are a student or write a lot of letters, a printer will be a wise investment. There are generally three types of printers. **Letter-quality printers** are high quality printers, but are costly and slow. **Dot matrix printers** are faster, but do not print as well. Want both speed and quality? A **Laser printer** is what is needed, but a fat price tag will come with it.

Modems

Another handy item to go along with your computer is a MODULATOR/DEMODULATOR, or just simply a **modem**. A modem makes your computer act like a telephone. It uses phone lines to send and receive information from other computer systems. You have probably seen people talk to each other by computer or have heard about people paying their bills through computer - this is all done with modems. A modem can be loads of fun (see "Your Own Thang" chapter), but before you buy one, there are some things you should know. First, make sure your modem is **"Hayes compatible"**. The Hayes company created a modem that became the industry's standard, and many communication arenas require "Hayes compatibility." So check that out before writing a check! Another issue is modem speed. The speed of a modem is measured by baud rate. Baud rate measures the amount of data being transferred or sent per second. Most users use 1200 baud or 2400 baud modems. Businesses generally have more data to transmit, so 9600 baud modems are common. Prices for 1200 baud and 2400 baud modems range from $60-$200.

OTHER PERIPHERALS

There are dozens of other items to add to your PC. A **mouse** is a small device connected to your computer by wire. Mice are very popular in drawing programs and programs that involve a lot of cursor movement (like Wordprocessors or Spreadsheets). A **scanner** is a device used to bring illustrations into computers. Drawings and black and white photographs can be easily scanned into many Desktop Publishing programs and other graphic programs. A Joy stick, which is used for games, is another popular peripheral. Many PC games have keyboard options, but **Joy Sticks** will give you the best feel for many arcade games.

THE PRACTICAL APPROACH

You do not have to buy all at once. You can start with a basic system and build up. Take a practical approach. I like to think of my friend, Pierre, who bought a basic stereo system a few years ago: a turntable, cassette player, and two feeble speakers. He could not immediately afford a system with a lot of power and accessories. But every few months Pierre added to his system. Now he has an amplifier, equalizer, echo box, compact disk, and large, booming speakers throughout his apartment. To say the least, Pierre's place is now the "spot," and everyone is in awe of his sound system. This is the same way you can build your PC. You can start small, with an XT that has expansion capabilities so you can add equipment. I started with an XT, added a Hard Drive, changed the monitor, bought a printer, added a 3.5" disk, bought a mouse, nabbed a modem and got a faster microprocessor (80286) in one year! I am not yet the "Pierre of PCs," but I could not afford all this when I first began. So check this option out, and do not be discouraged if you cannot afford the latest models. The important thing is just to get one (and get paid!).

CHAPTER 7

SOFTWARE

The collective term for programs and applications (WordPerfect, Lotus) is **software.** Without software your PC is nothing but a narrow box in your living room. Software and hardware work together to create the personal computer phenomenon. We have discussed hardware, so what about software? We have discussed the Big 3, but there are thousands of software programs in the PC world. Arcade games, musical programs, Biblical applications, home banking, typing tutorial programs— these are only a few packages within the wide range of PC software programs available.

WHERE TO GET SOFTWARE?

Retail Outlets

ComputerLand, **Egghead Software**, **SoftWherehouse**, and **800 Software** are major retailers that have all the popular and not-so-popular programs. They also have experts to answer questions and help you test software programs before purchasing them. These are also good places to browse software or just "window shop." You never know what you may find.

Shareware

Retail Outlets tend to carry big-name software companies' products (like Microsoft), and their prices may make you pause. Shareware programs are programs that are made by smaller businesses or individual programmers. If money is a problem, their prices are the biggest attraction. For instance, you can buy a database program like PC-File 5.0 for less than $150, while popular database programs like DBASE IV run around $500 (remember, learning the concept is what is most important). They call it Shareware because Shareware developers encourage users to "share" or give copies to your friends. And if they like it, they should send money to the author. This method is unique because most software companies require payment first and do not encourage copying.

Where do you get Shareware? **On-line services, computer bulletin boards, computer user groups, and shareware mail-order houses** are the primary sources. Using your modem, you can **download** information from On-line services that offer Shareware programs. **Genie** and **CompuServe** are big national On-line services. **Shareware Mail Order** houses have the latest programs direct from the developer. Most will have catalogs that you can order first and browse through. If you decide to join a **PC User Group,** check out their User Group Library. This is a collection of Shareware programs that members have access to. (See Appendix C for more information on Shareware.)

CAUTION: *Viruses!*

It does matter where you get Shareware programs, mainly because "viruses" are sometimes attached to the program. Viruses are hidden human-made programs that "infect" disks. Some viruses cause no harm, but others may have malign effects like erasing data or displaying nasty messages on your screen. Sharing programs that have been in other people's machines increases the possibility of getting a virus. So try to obtain Shareware from main channels, instead of friends or computer nerds. The main channels are taking every possible step to bring standards to this wide-open system. The Association of Shareware Professionals is an organization of Shareware developers that has standard consumer practices. So to be safe, check if the Shareware developer belongs to this organization.

ANOTHER WORD ABOUT SOFTWARE . . .

When you begin shopping for software, you will notice **version numbers.** For instance, "WordPerfect 5.1" has nothing to do with fractions, but is interpreted as "major version five, first minor revision." Why is this necessary? Well, before

WordPerfect 5.1 there was WordPerfect 5.0 and WordPerfect 4.2. The "5" shows that it has had a major development change (which it did!). The "1" shows that version 5.0 had a minor revision, which usually means bugs or minor errors are fixed.

As a software consumer, you also should look into registering your software with the maker. Many software packages come with user registration cards that usually entitle users to future announcements, developments, and **upgrades** (newer versions).

CHAPTER 8

YOUR OWN THANG...

If you were to call me "computer nerd," we may have to fight, but there are times when I just cannot get off my computer. At home, I do not feverishly practice Spreadsheet or Database Management, but I do like to explore the boundless world of computing. Games, Education, and Communication activities are many PC users' favorite computer pastimes. The versatility of a PC has made it very attractive to people of all walks of life. I have seen everyone, from rap DJs avidly pursuing musical programs for a gig, to ministers seeking out Biblical software for a sermon. I encourage you to look into PC software and consider your personal interest, because money is not everything. You will discover that besides keeping you occupied on a Friday night, a PC may help you discover an interest you never thought you had.

GAMES

I love arcade games, and the PC has so many arcade games that I don't even worry about buying a Nintendo. Action games made by Electronic Arts are my favorite. Their **John Madden Football**, **Lakers vs. Celtics** (Basketball), and **Earl Weaver Baseball** simulate real life athletes and can really get a sports fan wound up. I may have finished this book a bit earlier if I didn't play them so much. Besides sports action games, strategy and adventure games have been known to keep users in suspense for hours. Dungeons 'n Dragons is a popular adventure game, and the computer version is tremendous! Strategy games like Chess and Poker are also available.

EDUCATION

Many people may think that computer education programs are an issue only for kids and students. But the educational software markets can be of interest to non-students too. Whether it's practicing typing, improving your writing, or learning a foreign language, a computer education program can help you pursue your personal interests. Computer educational programs are famous for tracking your progress, using solid drills, building real-life models, without ever getting tired. But the best feature is that you can learn at your own pace.

There are also ethnic educational programs available. AfroLink Software **Afri-American Insight 1.2** is a comprehensive Black Information program. It has tons of data on Black colleges, Black Mayors, African-American businesses and much more. All of us who have an interest in our progress will find this program useful and informative.

COMMUNICATIONS

If you decide to get a modem, you can open your computer to another world. Remember, a modem acts like a telephone and lets you call up other computer systems. This enables you to pay bills, check news events, play games, and even have your groceries delivered! On-line services like Prodigy, CompuServe, and Genie have all these features. In Prodigy you can check the score of the basketball game, do some shopping, participate in the User Group discussions, and then check tomorrow's weather all in one session. Many On-line services charge by the minute, but Prodigy has unlimited use for a low monthly rate. African-American interests can also be found by modem communications. AfroLink **CPTime** is an On-line service that provides forums on worldwide Black issues. This is also a great place to meet people with similar interest and exchange ideas.

CHAPTER 9

SCHOOL DAZE!

THE SCENE

Going to school definitely has its advantages, and obtaining solid computer skills is definitely one of them. Using computers in school will be immediately advantageous in your educational efforts, but it also will help you in your professional development. Computer skills are becoming more in demand for internships and post-graduation jobs. Many colleges offer introductory computer courses that cover the Big 3 applications. If you are a student, try to integrate a class into your schedule. Also, you can tap into the campus on-line community and talk to other students via modem at other campuses. This is a popular way to converse with other people (professors too) in the academic arena. Check your school's computer department about obtaining an account. For a college student, your opportunity to become a skilled computer user is great. And with college cost rising, computer skills may yield the best return on your educational investment.

STUDENT SAVINGS

As described in the "Finding Computers" chapter, schools are the primary place to get, access, and find computers, but also another great place to buy computer hardware and computer software. **IBM** and **Apple** have flooded the educational market and sell their systems at a notable discount to students. For example, an IBM PC with a 30 megabyte Hard Drive and 286 microprocessor retails for $1500. But IBM student discounts range from 15% to 20% off the retail price. Also, IBM student packages often include software. Microsoft Windows, Microsoft Word for Windows, Microsoft Excel for Windows can also be obtained with a student-purchased IBM PC at extreme discounts. Apple also has a notable student mark-down on its computers; notably, the Macintosh Classic with a Hard Drive retails for about $1300, but students can swipe one for about a cool $1000. There also student loans available to purchase

Apple and IBM computers. Students or parents can take out loans if they meet minimal requirements and repay monthly. See your school's computer center for Apple and IBM loan requirements.

Buying software separately is another student advantage. Microsoft, Wordperfect, and Lotus are a few of the many software makers that have special student discounts. Microsoft Word retails for about $450, but students may be able to get a copy for less than $150. But there are some software packages that have student edition restrictions. Student Editions may not offer all the features as the regular version. Some makers may not offer phone technical support or may sell the program without some advanced features (features that students do not have the need for). For instance, a spreadsheet program may shrink the worksheet by not offering the maximum number of columns and rows. These Student Edition restrictions keep businesses and non-students from purchasing software at great student discounts.

To look into student savings, check school bookstores or school computer departments. Some larger campuses may even have special computer or electronic stores that have this information on display.

GETTING PAID

Getting computer supplies is not the only advantage for students. Student status also helps in finding jobs. Many employers aggressively recruit students to work. A student with computer skills is often a big plus to employers. Students tend to be more flexible and energetic. Also, they usually have medical and health benefits through their parents or school. Employers will gladly pay $8/hr-$15/hr. to have this combination rather than seek out professionals who may demand higher salary and benefits. Wordprocessing, Data Entry, and Database Management are a few jobs I did while in college. Even though

I made good money, I knew I was a bargain. College job boards are filled with positions requiring computer skills, and while you get paid you will build a solid resumé. It may not be a plus to tell GE or Xerox after graduation that you served pizza or loaded boxes into trucks for four (or five) years, when others will be telling recruiters what they already know about professional environments.

But don't be confined to working for others. As a student your flexible schedule, coupled with good computer skills, may help you start "your own thang." Resumé services, typing services, and other student demands could be big business on the college scene. Or just sit back and explore what you would really like to plug into, like art, music, or even publishing (hhhmmm!).

CHAPTER 10

THE APPLE MAC

MAC-PC DEBATE

Once you thrust yourself into the computer arena, you will soon hear the ongoing debate between PC users and Apple Macintosh users. This debate has taken a few twists through the years, and there are definitely more to come. Early in the debate it was said that the Mac had better graphics, but the PC is more powerful. Now both are comparable since VGA monitors have improved PC graphics and Motorola microprocessors have given the Mac punch. Another issue is price. Clones have greatly helped the PC consumer by providing quality PCs at low prices. But no one has yet cloned the Mac, and Apple is the only maker, so low competition has meant higher prices. Recently, Apple responded to the criticism by slashing prices dramatically and introducing the Mac Classic. The Mac Classic is their cheapest computer, retailing at around $1000. But even at this price there is still criticism.

EASIER?

The biggest issue in the debate is "which one is easier to use?" Mac users boast about the **icon** features. What is this? Instead of displaying characters on the screen, the Mac uses graphic images to illustrate a program. For instance, a wordprocessing program may be represented by a paper and pencil icon or graphic symbol. So, instead of typing the wordprocessing program, you can use the mouse to "point and click" on the icon. Also, the Mac features pull-down menus that contain all the Mac functions. If you want to save or open a file, then you select the FILE menu and a list of functions will appear. It also has an EDIT menu that lets you copy, cut, and paste files or specific data. But its most admired feature is **windows.** A window is what displays the application (like a wordprocessing program) you are working on. The Mac allows you to work on several windows at once. So you can display your Wordprocessor, Database, and Spreadsheet simultaneously.

PC RESPONSE

Some Apple Macintosh features have made the PC world really take note. The PC 3.5" inch diskettes and mouse peripheral were first used by Apple. Microsoft Windows is now the latest PC craze (more in "Doing Windows" chapter). Windows is a PC program that has many of the same features that were originally only on the Mac. Now PC users can use pull-down menus, click on icons, and pull up several programs at once. These developments are beginning to make both machines similar and bring a standard to personal computers.

Though the Mac is making waves throughout the computer industry, PC computers dominate the market. And if you want to get paid, chances are that many businesses are using a PC, and PC skills are essential. The Mac is newer and it took some time before business software was made for it, so the PC has had a head start. However, the Mac does have a strong following, and it is not a bad idea to learn it too.

GETTING PAID: MAC STYLE!

There are businesses that do prefer the Mac over the PC. Businesses that emphasize graphics are one. Remember that Apple graphics were overwhelmingly favored to PCs a few years ago. Here, Desktop Publishing programs like Aldus Pagemaker is a favorite. For many Mac wordprocessing jobs Microsoft Word is required. Microsoft Excel is the most desired Spreadsheet program. And the Microsoft Works (See Integrated Packages in Big 3 Chapter) database is usually used for Database Management. All these programs are available on the PC too, so if you buy a Mac, remember not to buy the PC version.

CHAPTER 11

DOING WINDOWS

You may not do glass windows, but many people are doing **Microsoft Windows**. What is Windows? Windows was introduced to change PC computing from a character-based to a graphics-based environment. As mentioned in "The Apple Mac" chapter the PC and Apple worlds are always competing. One plus on the Apple side was its graphical interface and graphic images, which made many PC users jealous. Windows was introduced in response to that, and it has had an extreme impact on the personal computer market. Now, the PC has a graphics environment and is giving PC users many advantages which previously were available only to Apple Macintosh users.

LOOKING THROUGH WINDOWS

The Windows package runs at about $100 or less and comes with a number of features. It has a communications program, paint program, wordprocessor, calculator, calendar, file management area, and many others. Its popularity has forced software makers to make **"...for Windows"** packages or software packages that run under the Windows' environment (graphical interface). For, instance there is **Microsoft Word** and **Microsoft Word for Windows.** Microsoft Word runs only on the regular DOS environment and Word for Windows on Windows. Another Windows feature is **multitasking:** you can balance a budget with a Spreadsheet in one window, type a report with a wordprocesor in another, and see it all! Then you can use **cut, paste,** and **copy** features to put your Spreadsheet data into the wordprocessor document.

I have to admit, I like the Windows environment. I especially like **WYSIWYG**. What is WYSIWYG? It stands for "What You See Is What You Get." Specifically, this means that what you see on your computer screen is how it will be printed on paper. When you use regular DOS programs, the display comes in one standard look. For example, when you want to *italicize* or make bigger letters, you usually have to wait until the program is printed. I started this book using **WordPerfect** (for DOS), but fell in love with **Microsoft Word for Windows** when I began to actually see my product on screen instead of having to print it out first!

A WINDOW OF OPPORTUNITY

Though Windows is very popular, it is still fairly new to most PC users. But it is starting to gain acceptance in businesses and "doing Windows" will soon mean jobs. All the popular and not-so popular software makers are adding "...for Windows" versions. Big 3 Windows' applications has already begun to gain corporate acceptance, so watch the want ads!

You can also take it a step further. Consultants are making big dollars teaching Windows. Businesses are and will be needing people to help retrain there staffs on Windows. Consultant training courses may run close to $1000, but it is not unusual for them to command $150/hr - $250/hr rate. Do I recommend the consultant courses route? If you are a go-getter type and can see the Windows demand in your geographical area, do it! Microsoft University has classrooms in many major U.S. cities, and beginners and advanced courses are available.

CHAPTER 12

The best way to start to become a sound PC user is to learn DOS. What is DOS? DOS is a collection of programs that manages the flow of data in and out of the PC and manages data on disks. DOS stands for Disk Operating System. In other words, *DOS is runnin' thangs!* However, not all PC users have sharp DOS skills. So why learn it? Because DOS is standard on every PC, and it exposes you to many computer basics. Copying files, erasing files, checking file size, and other file management techniques are available in DOS. Also, chances are that not every business or job requiring PC skills will have Lotus or WordPerfect, but they will have DOS! And a quick way to show you have solid PC skills is to know DOS well.

One reason why PC users do not learn DOS well is because many programs try to make DOS invisible by putting DOS commands (like Copy) in their programs. For example, a user can copy files in WordPerfect as well as in DOS. For my first few years of PC computing I did not work in DOS because I did not think it was important since other programs had common DOS functions. But when I decided to get serious about getting paid, everyone recommended DOS books. I wondered why because I did not see many jobs that required DOS expertise only. Most, in fact, required the Big 3 applications. Reluctantly, I learned DOS with the Big 3. I then became a confident user when I was able to manage files and do a couple of DOS tricks! I was so comfortable that I quickly grasped the concepts of the Big 3. But it should be remembered that while DOS alone may not get you to the bank immediately, it does provide the best groundwork for building your PC skills.

CHAPTER 13

LAST WORDS

So now you have it—an inside guide to personal computers and a few ways to get paid. Where should you start?...At a bookstore? Computer outlet? School? If you are anxious (like I was) to start making money, then you should check out the job listings in your area. Most likely you will see at least one Big 3 application. The strategy I used was to learn the most demanded first. So if you see applications like WordPerfect in demand, check schools and bookstores for instruction.

EMPLOYMENT

Also, while you're taking a class or learning computer skills, do not be afraid to apply for computer-related positions. I have found that if you are honest and tell employers what you know and what you are learning, you still have a solid chance. And if you are hired and continue to develop into a skilled computer user, you have shown determination and progress (good employee characteristics)!

Once you land a position, try to continue to learn more computer skills. I am not suggesting that you strive for "nerdiness," but look into learning more demanded computer software applications. For instance, the first Database I learned was dBASE. A few months later I landed a job that had Paradox (another popular database program). I didn't have to know Paradox for my position, but I started fiddling with it because I remembered other jobs that had required Paradox experience. I am glad I did because I left that company after a few short months and found a better job that asked for Paradox experience. If you continue to sharpen your skills, you will increase your marketability and help you find other jobs. I have far too many friends who hate their jobs, but none of them are quitting. Why? Because they have no marketable skills. Even after acquiring computer skills I still have had to work for a few jerks —but not for long!

FEAR

The day I finally decided to write this book was after a young African-American woman told me, "I'm afraid of computers, Eno." She typed a startling 65 wpm and would not apply for a job because it requested WordPerfect skills. I gasped and realized that something needed to be said.

Most people are afraid of the unknown. And computers, for many African-Americans, is the unknown mainly because it has not yet been introduced to us by our own people. To conquer that fear remember that a computer is just a human-made tool for humans. Like a hammer to carpenter or clippers to a barber, a computer is used to perform specific tasks. After some thought I realized that I, too, was somewhat afraid of computers, primarily because I was afraid of change. For many of us, computer-related jobs were not something our parents did. We are definitely living in a new era. Again, I encourage you to get support in obtaining computer skills, because we all are in a sense pioneers.

GO!

Don't procrastinate learning computers. Now is the perfect time. Do not do (everything) like me and wait until your financial security is in jeopardy or you run out of options. I was lucky. It is best to do it when things are steady and time is plenty. Experts predict that America's job market will continue to change. Many of the jobs (requiring low skills) that we African-Americans now have will decrease in the coming years.

Finally, I encourage those who are computer skilled to offer support to those who are not. As African-Americans we may agree that we are at a time where togetherness is needed, because "divided we fall, together we get paid!"

PEACE.

NATIONAL BDPA CHAPTERS

Akron Chapter
BDPA
P.O. Box 8288
Akron, OH 44320

Atlanta Chapter
BDPA
P.O. Box 50462
Atlanta, GA 30302-9998

Baltimore Chapter
BDPA
P.O. Box 31605
Baltimore, MD 21207

Bay Area Chapter
BDPA
Suite 197
2625 Alcatraz Ave.
Berkeley, CA 94705

Central Arkansas Chapter
BDPA
c/o Levita Cleveland
11701 Mara Lynn #132
Little Rock, AK 72211

Charlotte Chapter
BDPA
P.O. Box 36662
Charlotte, NC 28236

Chicago Chapter
BDPA
P.O. Box 16490
Chicago, IL 60616-0548

Cincinnati Chapter
BDPA
P.O. Box 429215
Cincinnati, OH 45242-9215

Cleveland Chapter
BDPA
P.O. Box 91082
Cleveland, OH 44101-3082

Colorado Springs Chapter
BDPA
P.O. Box 62181
Colorado Springs, CO 80962

Columbus Chapter
BDPA
P.O. Box 29170
Columbus, OH 43229

Dallas Chapter
BDPA
P.O. Box 815783
Dallas, TX 75381

Dayton Chapter
BDPA
P.O. Box 0831
Dayton, OH 45401-0831

Detroit Chapter
BDPA
65 Cadillac Sq.
Suite 3200
Detroit, MI 48226

Ft. Wayne Chapter
BDPA
P.O. Box 12672
Ft. Wayne, IN 46864

Greenville Chapter
BDPA
P.O. Box 26416
Greenville, SC 29616

Hartford Chapter
BDPA
P.O. Box 2522
Hartford, CT 06146

Houston Chapter
BDPA
P.O. Box 772145
Houston, TX 77215-2145

Indianapolis Chapter
BDPA
P.O. Box 44509
Indianapolis, IN 46204

Jacksonville Chapter
BDPA
c/o Alonzo Howell
11654 Jackman Cove Lane
Jacksonville, FL 32218

Kansas City Chapter
BDPA
P.O. Box 414844
Kansas City, MO 64141

Los Angeles Chapter
BDPA
P.O. Box 94393
Pasadena, CA 91109

Mass/Metrowest Chapter
BDPA
P.O. Box 1045
Northboro, MA 01532

Memphis Chapter
BDPA
P.O. Box 30483
Memphis, TN 38130-0483

Northern New Jersey Chapter
BDPA
P.O. Box 22851
Newark, NJ 07101

New Orleans Chapter
BDPA
P.O. Box 57656
New Orleans, LA 70157

New York Chapter
BDPA
P.O. Box 808
Murry Hill Stn
New York, NY

Oklahoma City Chapter
BDPA
c/o Jacqulin R. Washington
2301 N.W. 109 St.
Oklahoma City, OK 73120

Philadelphia Chapter
BDPA
P.O. Box 2254
Philadelphia, PA 19103

Phoenix Chapter
BDPA
c/o Larry Johnson
5125 N. 16th St. #A112
Phoenix, AZ 85016-0142

Pittsburgh Chapter
BDPA
P.O. Box 7494
Pittsburgh, PA 15213

South Jersey
BDPA
P.O. Box 2126
Willingboro, NJ 08046

Springfield Chapter
BDPA
P.O. Box 90906
Springfield, MA 01139

St. Louis Chapter
BDPA
P.O. Box 952
Florissant, MO 63033

Tallahassee Chapter
BDPA
c/o Malcolm Barnes
3130 Ferns Glen Dr.
Tallahassee, FL 32308

Triangle Chapter
BDPA
4th Floor
101 City Hall Plaza
Durham, NC 27701

Tri Cities Chapter
BDPA
c/o Rita Swan
2181 Finch Dr.
Saginaw, MI 48601-5730

Toledo Chapter
BDPA
P.O. Box 1078
Toledo, OH 43697-1078

Twin Cities Chapter
BDPA
P.O. Box 40204
St. Paul, MN 55104-9998

Washington D.C. Chapter
BDPA
P.O. Box 2420
Washington, D.C. 20013

Wilmington Chapter
BDPA
P.O. Box 26037
Wilmington, DE 19899

MAGAZINES

PC Magazine
Subscription
PO Box 51833
Boulder, CO 80321-1524

MacWorld
Subscription Dept
PO Box 51666
Boulder, CO 80321-1666

PC Novice
PO Box 85380
Lincoln, NE 68501-9815

MacUser
Subscription Dept
Box 52461
Boulder, CO 80321-2461

PC World
Subscription
PO Box 51833
Boulder, CO 80321-1833

Byte
Subscription Dept.
Box 558
Highstown, NJ 08520-9409

SHAREWARE

The following is a listing of where you can obtain Shareware programs. You may contact these organizations to send their Shareware order catalogs:

Association of Personal Computer User Groups
1101 Conneticut Ave.
NW #901
Washington, DC
20036

Association of Shareware Professionals
P.O. Box 5786
Bellevue, WA 98006

Public Software Library
P.O. Box 35705
Houston, TX 77235
800-242-4775

PC-SIG
1030 E. Duane Ave. Ste D
Sunnyvale, CA 94086
800-245-6717

·Public Brand Software
Box 51315
Indianapolis, IN

PRODUCT INFORMATION

AFRI-INSIGHT and
CPTime ONLINE
AfroLink Software
1815 Wellington Rd.
Los Angeles, CA 90019
213-732-1923

MACINTOSH
Apple Computer Inc.
Cupertino, CA
800-776-2333

CompuServe
1-800-848-8199

dBASE
Ashton-Tate
20101 Hamilton Ave.
Torrance, CA
800-437-4329

EARL WEAVER
BAEBALL,
JOHN MADDEN FOOT-
BALL
and LAKERS vs. CELTICS
Electronic Arts
800-448-8822

EXCEL, WORD, WORKS,
WINDOWS, and QUICK C
Microsoft Corp
Redmond, WA
206-882-8080

EXPRESS PUBLISHER
Power Up Software
Corporation
2929 Campus Dr.
San Mateo, CA 94403
415-345-2662

FOXBASE
Fox Software
134 W. South Boundary
Perrysburg, OH 43551
419-874-0162

LOTUS 1-2-3
Lotus Development Corp
Cambridge, MA
617-577-8500

PC-FILE
Buttonware
P.O. Box 96058
Bellevue, WA 98009
800-528-8866

PAGEMAKER
Aldus Corporation
411 First Ave. Ste #200
Seattle, WA 98104
206-622-5500

PFS FIRST CHOICE
Spinnaker
1 Kendall Square
Cambridge, MA 02139
617-494-1200

TYPING INSTRUCTOR Encore
Individual Software, Inc
5870 Stoneridge Inc.
Pleasonton, CA 94588

TYPING TUTOR
Simon & Schuster Software
125 Shoreway Road
Suite 3000
San Carlos, CA
800-331-3313

VENTURA
Xerox Corp.
101 Continental Blvd.
El Segundo, CA
800-822-8221

WORDPERFECT
WordPerfect Corp
288 Center St.
Orem, UT 84057
801-227-5000

GLOSSARY

A

APPLE — Computer company that makes the MACINTOSH.

B

BASIC — Computer programming language geared primarily toward beginners.

BOOT — The term for starting up the computer.

BPS — A measure of speed which a device (i.e. like a modem) can send or receive data.

BUG — An error in software or hardware.

BULLETIN BOARD SYSTEMS (BBS) — A computer system with one or more modems that serves as an information center for dial-up users.

BYTE — A single character, such as the letter 'a'.

C

CAD — Stands for Computer Aided Design which are popular programs for Architects, Engineers.

COLUMNS (Spreadsheets) — A series of items arranged vertically. Usually specified by letters.

CLONE — A copy; the term "PC clone" means that the computer is compatible to the IBM PC.

CPU — Stands for Central Processing Unit a.k.a microprocessor; brain of computer; interprets and processes data.

D

DATA — An item of information.

DATABASE — Collection of data consisting of records, that is useful to search, store, and sort.

dBASE — A top database program. Great one to learn for employment.

DISKETTE — see FLOPPY DISK.

DOWNLOAD — The process of transferring data from a remote computer to a local computer by modem.

DOS — A group of programs that manage the data on disk and control the flow in and out of the PC.

DOT MATRIX PRINTER — A printer that uses "tiny" dots to form characters and letters.

E

EXPANSION SLOTS — Sockets located inside the computer that allows users to add adapter cards in order to perform more functions (i.e. joysticks, printers, modems, etc.).

EXPRESS PUBLISHER — A top Desktop Publishing program.

F

FILE — A collection of data grouped under one name.

FILENAME — Name given to a file.

FIXED DISK —see Hard Disk.

FLOPPY DISK — Used to store data from floppy disk drive. Comes in 3.5 inch and 5.25 inch formats for PC. Storage sizes range from a few hundred thousand bytes to over 1 million bytes.

FLOPPY DISK DRIVE — An electromechanical device that reads and writes data to floppy disks.

H

HARD DISK DRIVE — a.k.a. Fixed Disk; read and writes data to an already stored disk. Hard Disks tend to have more of a storage capacity. PC storage typical range from 20 megabytes to over a gigabyte.

HARDWARE — The actual physical parts of a computer system (i.e. monitor, disk drive, printers).

I

INTEGRATED PACKAGES — Application programs that combine several different tasks such as word processing, database management, and spreadsheets.

J

JOYSTICK — A control device primarily used for video games.

K

KILOBYTE — 1000 bytes or characters (i.e. 1000 'l').

L

LASER PRINTER — A printer that uses the same technology as a photocopier.

LETTER QUALITY PRINTER — A printer that produces characters similar to a typewriter.

LOTUS 1-2-3 — A popular Spreadsheet Program — LEARN IT!

M

MEGABYTE — 1 million bytes; 1 million characters; 1 million 'l'.

MEMORY — In personal computers this primarily refers to RAM (Random Access Memory) which holds data only while the computer is on.

MICROSOFT WORD — A top wordprocessing program.

MODEM — A device that makes your computer act like a telephone, giving it the ability to call other computers.

MONOCHROME — Refers to monitors that display images in one color.

MICROPROCESSOR — The "heart" or "brain" of a computer. PC microprocessors are the 8088, 8086, 80286, 80386, 80386SX, 80486 and 80486SX.

MOTHERBOARD — The main circuit board containing the main components of a computer.

MOUSE — A pointing device used to limit the amount of keyboard strokes.

O

OUTPUT — The data sent from the computer to the screen or printer.

P

PAGEMAKER — Top Desktop Publishing program.

PERIPHERALS — Additional devices (printer, mouse, joysticks) that are not essential to the operation of the program.

PROMPT —The location indicator showing that the computer is ready for input.

PUBLISH IT! — A great Desktop Publishing program at a cheap price.

R

RAM — Acronym for Random Access Memory; generally refers to computer memory.

ROM — Acronym for Read Only Memory; ROM chips have programs permanently written on them.

ROWS (Spreadsheet) — A group of items arranged horizontally. Usually specified by numbers.

S

SPREADSHEET PROGRAM — Software that performs calculations and displays data in a ledger format.

T

TYPING INSTRUCTOR — A great instructional typing program.
TYPING TUTOR — A top typing program.

U

UPGRADE — Refers to a newer version of a software or hardware product.
UPLOAD — The process of transferring data from a local computer to a remote computer by modem.

W

WORKSHEET — The data area of a computer spreadsheet program.
WORDPERFECT — A top wordprocessing program. Visible in a lot of businesses.
WORD PROCESSOR — Application program for printing text-based documents.

V

VGA — Acronym for Video Graphics Array refers to monitor type.

INDEX

The Black Computer Survival Guide would not have been possible without the advice, support, and encouragement of these individuals and establishments:

AfroLink Software
Anderson, Bob
Baccus, Joe
BDPA BAC
Bishop, Angela
Buckley, Stacie
Campbell, Nadine
Clifton, Don
Dawan, Wesley
DTI
Glass, April
Hale, Steven
Hamilton, Keena
Jones, Pat
Kobler, Helmut
Kreig, Michael
Lewis, Alex
Lundeen and Associates

Marcus Books and Printing
McDow, Darren
Morishita, Heiji
Pressley, Kesha
Price, Reggie
Professor J. Lipps
Professor F. Schurmann
Railey, Olivia
Richardson, Billy
Scott, Chris
Smith, Alex
Still, Diana
Taylor, Karyn
Trent, Michael
Washburn, Gary
White, Ischmael
Willis, Nadia

ABOUT THE AUTHOR

Eno Essien is a 22-year old, 1992 University of California at Berkeley graduate in Economics. He was the Co-founder and President of the Black Student Data Processing Associates on the Berkeley campus. He has done computer-related work in several corporate arenas during his collegiate years which include insurance companies, consulting firms, software corporations, and several other professional organizations. But his biggest interest is to spark computer awareness in the African-American community.

ABOUT THE ARTIST

Heiji Morishita and the Author attended High School together in Los Angeles. Drawing is one of Heiji's favorite hobbies and he was happy to help enhance "The Guide." Heiji lives, works, and attends school in Los Angeles.

BLACKK INKK RESEARCH GROUP

Blackk Inkk Research Group is an upstart Publishing and Consulting company. Our primary goal is to address today's issues in the African-American community through the voices and visions of young, bright, and proud African-Americans. STAY TUNED FOR OUR NEXT RELEASE! Please feel free to send inquires, orders (check or money order)*, and letters to:

> Blackk Inkk Research Group
> 15 Golden Age Village
> P.O. Box 1682
> Emigrant, MT 59027
> 406-333-4523
> 510-839-7406

* Shipping is $3 for first book, $1.50 for each additional copy.